Copyright Page

AI-Generated Content Acknowledgement

This book contains content and imagery created with the assistance of OpenAI's ChatGPT, including editorial collaboration, structural formatting, and image generation.
All final content was curated, edited, and approved by the author.
Any AI-generated images are licensed for commercial use by the author and created explicitly for this publication.

Cover and Interior Design: James Miller - OpenAI's ChatGPT
ISBN: 979-8-89965-538-8

For permissions, questions, or speaking engagements:
Contact: j.c.miller@live.co.uk

Foreword

This book is not simply a record of personal awakening; it is a reflection of the collective shift unfolding in real-time.

What began as a solitary journey through emotional upheaval, systemic betrayal, and psychological fragmentation became a reclamation of inner truth, authenticity, and sovereignty.

When I first conceived **The Inversiverse**, it was an abstract concept, a mirror world that inverted everything I thought I knew. Over time, it became a sanctuary for exploration, where I could question everything: government, language, mental health, identity, belief, and selfhood.

As you read this book, you are not just reading about my experiences; you are meeting yourself in the margins. The pages are alive with questions meant to disrupt your programming, challenge your narratives, and restore your inner authority.

I offer this work not as doctrine, but as a doorway.

Enter with curiosity. Leave with clarity.

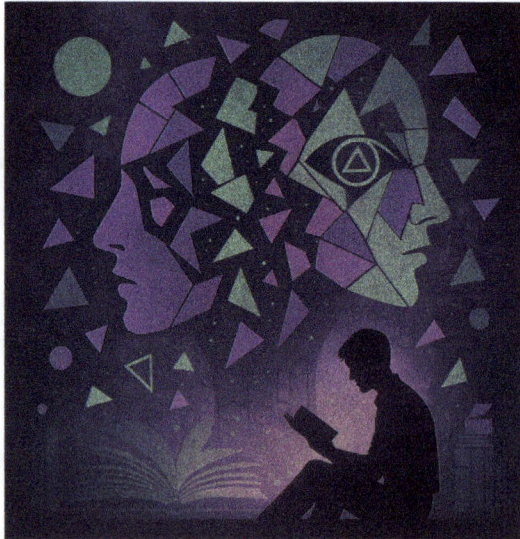

Preface

The idea for *The Inversiverse* was born in 2022, but its roots stretch much deeper, all the way back to 2015, when I was working as a Systems Engineer. I had just been promoted from a Test & Support Engineer role and became a STEM ambassador and mentor for others working towards professional registration through the Institute of Engineering and Technology (IET). I was proud of what I was achieving: gaining accreditation, working toward chartership, and ticking all the boxes in a career path that should have felt fulfilling.

But something didn't sit right. After two decades of education and engineering work, I realised that what I truly enjoyed wasn't the technical role itself, but helping others. Guiding them. Listening. Offering clarity. That realisation marked the beginning of a slow, profound transformation.

Eventually, I left the engineering world and retrained in mental health support, counselling, and coaching. I volunteered and later worked with the NHS, helping patients reintegrate into work after periods of illness. When the pandemic struck and the position was cut, I knew I couldn't abandon the path. I began creating content independently, weaving together everything I had experienced, both personally and professionally, into something new.

Between 2020 and 2023, I went through intense introspection and research. As someone living with autism, ADHD, and bipolar type II, I was determined to understand myself and others more deeply. I had to walk the talk, to ensure what I presented was authentic, lived, and congruent. I couldn't guide others if I hadn't done the work myself.

That work was messy. It was lonely. It brought me face-to-face with ego death, childhood trauma, emotional volatility, and spiritual awakening. In 2017, something in me burst open. My worldview collapsed. I felt misunderstood, accused of things that weren't true, abandoned by people I had once trusted, and yet, I also knew, deep down, that I had abandoned myself in the process of trying to "fit in."

I was no longer chasing a title or a salary. I was chasing the truth. I wasn't trying to be seen. I was trying to *see*, deeply, consciously.

The journey led me through dark valleys of confusion, procrastination, emotional chaos, and painful self-analysis. But it also gifted me with resilience, insight, and clarity. I came to realise that many of us are not broken, we are disoriented. We're not sick, we're spiritually malnourished. The systems around us do not serve our healing; they suppress it.

I no longer see life as a linear process of goals and outcomes. I live slower now. With intention. With space for reflection. I don't give away my energy to those who drain it. I take time to feel, to think, to connect inwardly. I've learned to recognise emotional manipulation, to break cycles of people-pleasing, and to stop giving my power away.

This book is not an instruction manual. It is not here to preach, convert, or claim superiority. It is a transmission. A mirror. A call to remember. If even one person reads these pages and feels seen, finds clarity, or gains the courage to step off the path that no longer serves them, then this entire journey will have been worth it.

Waking Up In A World Built To Keep You Asleep is a collection of insights, models, provocations, and offerings. It's for those who feel disoriented by modern life. For those who've sensed something is wrong but can't quite name it. For those who want to unlearn the noise and rediscover the signal, the true self beneath the static.

You don't need to become anything. You only need to remember.

Welcome to **The Inversiverse**.

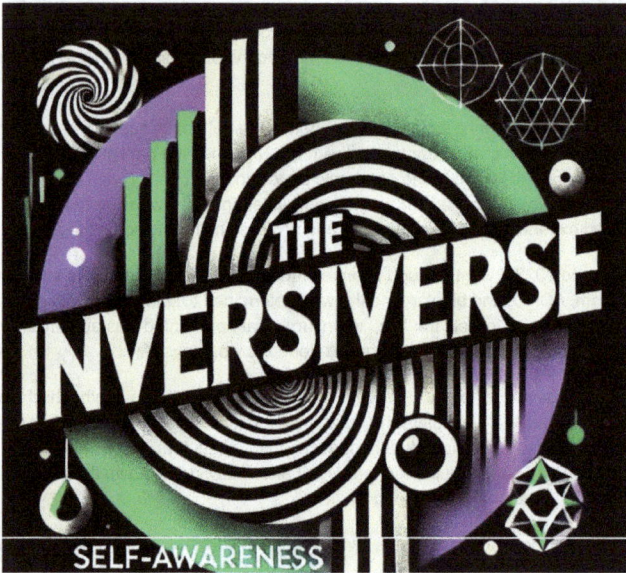

About the Author

James Miller, the author of *Waking Up In A World Built To Keep You Asleep,* is a former Electronics Systems Engineer who walked away from a two-decade-long career to pursue something more meaningful: understanding the self, unravelling social conditioning, and supporting others on their path to mental, emotional, and spiritual clarity.

With certifications in mental health, counselling, and coaching and a degree in Electronics & Communications, and lived experience of autism, ADHD, and bipolar type II, his work bridges lived truth and critical insight. After leaving a role in the NHS supporting those reintegrating into life after mental health struggles, he chose to create **The Inversiverse**, an independent series and philosophy exploring perception, indoctrination, trauma, identity, and personal sovereignty.

This book is not about fame, followers, or financial gain. It's an offering: an authentic, raw, and grounded account of what it means to dismantle illusion, confront ego, and rediscover purpose in a manipulated world.

The author lives a quiet life devoted to reflection, awareness, creativity, and truth, always questioning, always evolving, and always seeking to live in congruence with heart and mind.

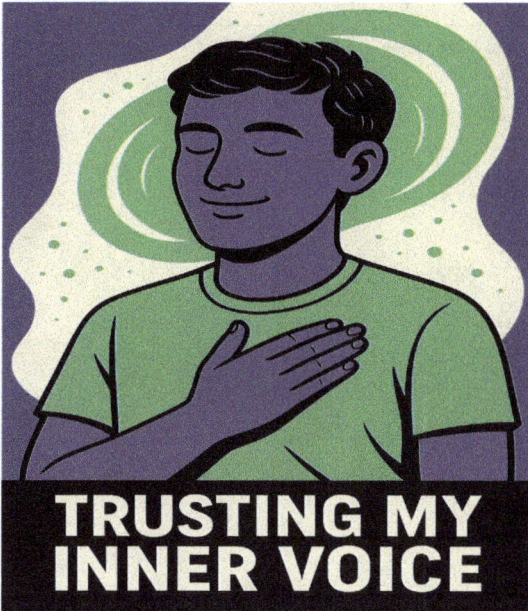

TRUSTING MY INNER VOICE

Part I: The Awakening

A personal and philosophical account of transformation through adversity, awakening, and emotional realignment.

1. **The Algorithmic Mind — Influence, Identity & Invisible Architects**
   Exploring programmed identity, memetics, social control systems, and the performance of self.

2. **Dark Psychology — The Occult Theatre**
   Unmasking gaslighting, symbolic control, emotional manipulation, and spiritual inversion.

3. **The Puppet Self — Social Scripts, Status Games & the Death of Authenticity**
   Identity performance, societal roles, and mimetic desire as described by thinkers like Goffman and Girard.

4. **Chemical Consent — Mental Health Medication, Perception & Emotional Conformity**
   The realities of psychiatric treatment, neurodivergence, emotional suppression, and pharmaceutical control.

Use This Space To Make Notes

Chapter 1: The Algorithmic Mind — Influence, Identity & Invisible Architects

You Are Not Who You Think You Are

You are who you were programmed to be.

That's not an insult. It's an invitation. A key to unlock something.

Most of what we call "identity" is simply the echo of external influence. The food we ate. The songs we heard. The fears we were taught. The words we were allowed to use. From birth, we are shaped. Not sculpted with care, but stamped like a product, mass-produced and categorised into marketable, manageable groups.

Our personalities are often reactionary: a quiet child becomes quieter in a loud world. A sensitive person becomes hardened by ridicule. A thinker learns to stay silent when the world punishes complexity. If you think you've made up your mind, you're likely mistaken. Unless you've gone through the painful process of unmaking it.

This is what I call the **Algorithmic Mind**, a psyche coded by invisible forces: family scripts, school lessons, state propaganda, pop culture, peer groups, emotional responses, likes, retweets, and targeted ads. A person whose sense of self is the result of endless feedback loops and emotional conditioning. A consciousness manipulated into compliance, in plain sight.

Memetics: The Virus of Ideas

Richard Dawkins coined the term "meme" to describe how cultural ideas replicate and evolve. A meme is not just an internet joke; it's an ideological fragment. It spreads from mind to mind like a virus, bypassing logic by embedding itself emotionally, visually, and symbolically.

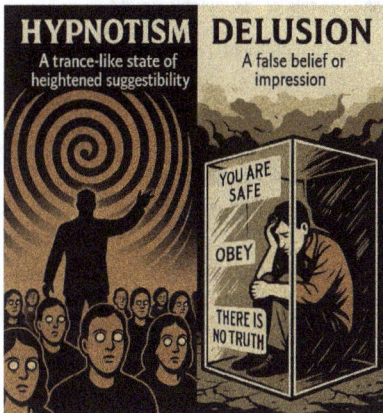

The Teenage Mutant Ninja Turtles were more than just characters. They were a *sensation*. One month, it was turtles. Then Pokémon. Then Beyblades. Then TikTok influencers. The cycles repeat. Each new craze is a new memetic injection: designed, launched, pushed, and later discarded. Behind it all, the same machinery: advertisers, producers, psychological marketers. And behind them? The architects.

7

Control Theory: The System of You

In engineering, control theory is the study of how to influence a system to behave in a desired way. It's about **inputs** and **feedback**. If you want a drone to fly a straight path, you adjust its behaviour through real-time data. If it drifts, you course-correct.

Now apply this to society. To people. To you.

Governments, corporations, media, and even schools all use control theory, whether they admit it or not. You were taught certain things were "normal." You were rewarded for good behaviour and punished for dissent. This wasn't a conspiracy. It was systemic conditioning.

We all live inside a cultural control system. The danger isn't that someone is at the helm. The danger is that we've stopped noticing it exists.

Invisible Architects: Who Writes Your Script?

Most people don't choose their identity. They *inherit* it. Or copy it. Or fall into it.

The ideas of who you should be, successful, masculine, feminine, desirable, professional, respectable, spiritual, were handed to you like costumes. Most people try them on and never take them off. Those who don't conform get labelled as unstable, rebellious, immature, or even mentally unwell.

And yet, those who have challenged the script often find the truth:

Identity is not a prison. It's a performance.

Erving Goffman wrote about the dramaturgical model of the self. Life is a stage. We wear masks. We play roles. We follow scripts. But who writes them?

In my case, I realised much of my early identity was about proving myself: achieving titles, getting recognition, climbing the ladder. I wasn't chasing my desires. I was running someone else's programme. I was just another actor playing the role of "acceptable adult."

Then I had my awakening. I stepped off the stage. And that's when I began to see the architects.

Algorithms of Belonging and Rejection

We all want to belong. But we also want to be authentic. The Algorithmic Mind traps us between the two. Say what you think, and you risk exile. Conform, and you abandon yourself.

Social media exploits this tension perfectly. Algorithms reward outrage, identity performance, and superficiality. The more tribal your behaviour, the more visible you become. The more nuanced or thoughtful your post, the less engagement it gets.

It's not just that the algorithm tracks your behaviour. It **shapes** it. And when your behaviour is shaped, your beliefs follow. This isn't a glitch in the system. This *is* the system.

8

Breaking the Loop

To break free from the Algorithmic Mind, you don't need to move to a cave or throw away your phone. You simply need to observe. To recognise when a thought, reaction, or belief doesn't belong to you.

Ask yourself:

- Where did this belief come from?
- Who benefits if I keep it?
- What am I afraid of losing if I let it go?

This book won't give you a new identity. It will help you dismantle the one that was given to you.

Because who you are doesn't need programming. It only needs remembering.

FROM PROGRAMMED TO PROGRAMMING

Integration Activity: Spot the Script

Over the next week, notice every time you use a label to describe yourself ("I'm just the type of person who...").

Then ask:

- Is that *you*?
- Or did someone once teach you that was who you should be?

You might be surprised at how many parts of your identity you never actually chose.

Use This Space To Make Notes

Chapter 2: Dark Psychology - The Occult Theatre

Behind the Curtain

Some illusions are so well-constructed, we live inside them. Others are so subtle, we deny they even exist. But the most dangerous illusions of all? The ones we're taught to *defend* with our minds, our reputations, and sometimes even our lives.

Dark psychology is not about magic. It's not about gothic cloaks or horror films. It's about power. The power to influence others through covert manipulation, emotional control, and behavioural conditioning. It's the psychological operating system beneath the surface of society, behind boardroom smiles, bureaucratic policies, religious sermons, and political speeches. Most of it is unseen. But not unintentional.

The Occult Theatre isn't some hidden basement ceremony. It's the public performance of deception, staged with symbols, language, and ritual. It is *everywhere*: in the courtroom, the newsroom, the classroom, the church. In every institution that claims moral authority, while disguising its true intention, **compliance**.

The Language of Reversal

Dark psychology often begins with *linguistic inversion*, the distortion of meaning to create confusion, compliance, or emotional disarmament. Words become weapons. Take phrases like:

- "Safe and effective"
- "For your good"
- "Trust the science"

These aren't always lies, but they often function as *emotional anchors*, phrases used to end questions, not inspire them. It's a form of mass spellcasting through suggestion and emotional priming. George Orwell warned of this in *1984* with "Newspeak": a language designed to limit thought by limiting vocabulary. What we cannot articulate, we cannot resist.

I noticed this in my own life, how debates and discussions were often shut down not by facts, but by *shame*, emotional appeals, or bureaucratic language. You don't question policy. You follow the procedure. You don't express hurt. You take medication. You don't resist. You conform.

This is how a society becomes pacified, not through violence, but through psychological seduction.

Gaslighting: The Institutional Kind

Most people associate gaslighting with abusive partners or narcissists. But institutions gaslight, too.

When authorities deny the obvious, rewrite history, or punish dissenters while claiming to support freedom, that is **collective gaslighting**. When systems claim to help but leave people worse off, while blaming the individual for not responding well enough, that, too, is institutional gaslighting.

I experienced this personally in the mental health system. The same system that claimed to support me offered medication that numbed me, dismissed my trauma, and judged my truth as instability. Their message: *"You are broken. We will fix you. But only if you submit to our terms."*

But I wasn't broken. I was fragmented. I wasn't delusional. I was awakening. And that distinction changes everything.

Symbolism & Psychological Anchors

The occult isn't about black magic. It's about hidden knowledge. And in our modern world, that knowledge is encoded in symbols. Corporations, governments, and religious institutions all use symbols to create emotional and behavioural associations, often without your awareness.

Why do so many powerful institutions use all-seeing eyes, pyramids, flames, and serpents? Because symbols bypass logic. They go straight to the subconscious. Like childhood stories or sacred rituals, they carry ancient emotional weight. When you see a uniform, a flag, or a sacred emblem, it triggers obedience, fear, and reverence, often without question.

These are *psychological anchors*, used to create automatic responses. The more emotionally charged a symbol is, the more powerful its effect. And when paired with repetition and ritual? It becomes religion, even if it's dressed as politics, education, or entertainment.

The Charm of the Predator

Here's a difficult truth: the most dangerous individuals don't wear warning signs. They are charming, articulate, intelligent, and highly strategic. We are taught to spot abusers as monsters. But real-world manipulators wear suits. They smile. They speak in polished tones. They apologise when exposed. They project empathy while exploiting trust.

This is the theatre. This is the act. And most people applaud, not knowing they are in the audience of their psychological enslavement. In the past, I noticed how I would overshare, hoping to be liked. I believed transparency would earn trust. But I learned the hard way, predators exploit openness. They probe your emotional needs, mirror your desires, and then shape your reality. Once you wake up to these patterns, you can't unsee them.

Seeing the Ritual for What It Is

The court system. The political campaign. The school exam. The celebrity scandal. The morning news. The anthem. The hand over the heart. The forced apology.

These are not just events. They are *rituals*. Repetitive symbolic acts are designed to reinforce a belief system. To make you feel part of something. To make dissent feel not only rebellious, but shameful. Once you see these rituals clearly, the illusion begins to crumble.

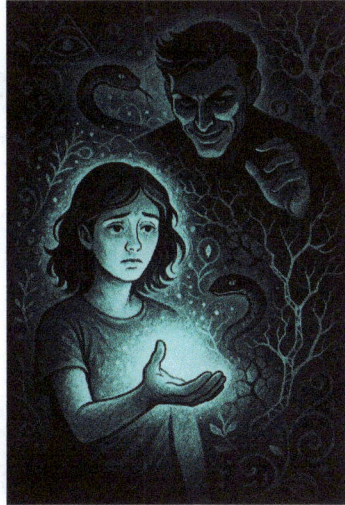

Cracks in the Mirror

Each of us experiences a unique inner reality, filtered through perception, memory, and imagination.

How much consensus is there in "consensus reality?"

Can we trust the reflected image?

Integration Activity: Decode a Ritual

Choose a weekly event you take part in or observe, a meeting, a ceremony, a media broadcast, a religious or political ritual.

Then ask:

- What symbols are present?
- What emotional tone is created?
- What behaviour is expected from participants?
- Who benefits from this ritual?

The goal isn't to dismiss all ritual; some are sacred and life-affirming. But to ask: *Who wrote this script?* And do I still choose to follow it?

Use This Space To Make Notes

Chapter 3: The Puppet Self — Social Scripts, Status Games & the Death of Authenticity

There is a self you show the world and a self that remains hidden, even from you.

Most people don't notice the mask. Not because it's invisible, but because it's *expected*.

From early childhood, we're given a script. "Be polite." "Speak when spoken to." "Act normal." We're taught how to smile even when we're sad. How to be agreeable even when we're angry. How to become palatable to others, even when it costs us authenticity.

We perform roles. At school, at work, online, at home. The "good student," the "dependable employee," the "funny friend," the "model parent." But rarely do we ask, who wrote these roles? And why do we perform them even when they hurt?

Goffman's Stage

Erving Goffman, a Canadian sociologist, described social life as a stage play. His "dramaturgical model" suggests that we are all actors performing roles in different contexts. We wear masks, not deceitfully, but out of necessity. Our "front stage" self is what we show to the world. Our "backstage" self is reserved, hidden, private, and often repressed.

Most of us have spent more time on the front stage than we realise. And in doing so, we forget who we are backstage.

I realised I had been performing for years. In relationships. At work. Even in moments of solitude, I caught myself narrating thoughts in a way that made them "make sense" to others, even if no one was listening. My identity was entangled in the need to be understood, liked, and validated. I gave away pieces of myself for approval, but the approval never lasted.

Status Games

We live in a world addicted to validation. Social media is the new colosseum, every post a performance, every like a token of approval. But behind the performances lies something more primal: a fight for status.

René Girard's theory of *mimetic desire* reveals that we don't just desire objects, we desire what others desire. We imitate one another's wants, which breeds rivalry, competition, and envy. We don't just want the car, or the partner, or the lifestyle; we want the recognition that comes with it.

And when we lose the game, when we feel unseen or irrelevant, we compensate. We exaggerate, edit, and posture. We develop what's been called the "false self", a curated identity built to win attention, not express truth.

But the cost of this game is enormous: the slow death of authenticity.

The Crisis of the Authentic Self

Authenticity is not about "being yourself" in every moment. It's about alignment. Congruence between what you feel, what you believe, and how you act. Most of us are taught to abandon that alignment early on.

We're told to pursue success, not meaning. To be agreeable, not truthful. To sacrifice honesty for harmony. And so we create selves that survive, but do not thrive.

For me, this came to a head during my professional transition. As a STEM ambassador and mentor, I found myself more fulfilled helping others than doing the technical work. Yet the identity I had constructed was built around achievement, recognition, and titles. Walking away felt like death, not of my career, but of the false self I had spent decades building.

It was painful. But it was necessary.

Unplugging from the Script

So, how do we step off the stage?

First, we need to identify the scripts we're following. Who taught you how to behave, what to value, who to be? Was it your parents? Teachers? Culture? A trauma response?

Second, we need to create space for discomfort. Dropping the mask can feel vulnerable. You may lose approval. You may lose people. But what you gain is a self you can live with.

Finally, we must permit ourselves to evolve. The self is not fixed. You're allowed to change your mind. To outgrow roles. To rewrite your story.

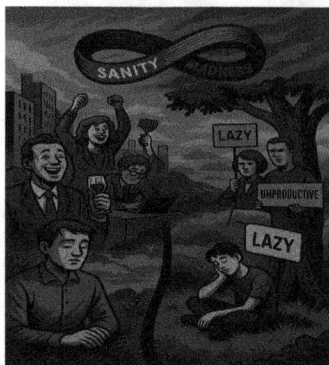

Integration Activity: De-Scripting the Self

1. **List five labels or roles you've been assigned in life.**
    (e.g., "the smart one," "the strong one," "the fixer," "the rebel," "the quiet one").

2. **For each role, ask yourself:**

    - Did I choose this?
    - Does it serve me?
    - What happens if I stop performing this role?

3. **Journal one scenario where you acted against your true feelings just to maintain a role.**
    Reflect on what it cost you, and what you might do differently now.

When we shed the puppet strings of social performance, we begin to move with our rhythm. Not for applause. Not for status. But from the quiet knowing that we are enough, as we are, as we feel, as we choose to be.

That is freedom. That is authenticity.

That is the return to self.

Use This Space To Make Notes

Chapter 4: Chemical Consent — Mental Health Medication, Perception & Emotional Conformity

The Pill That Promises Peace

Modern psychiatry often presents a simple formula: emotional distress equals chemical imbalance; chemical imbalance requires chemical correction. This is the narrative sold to millions, that depression, anxiety, mood fluctuations, or trauma responses can be pacified through pills. It is a story that appears scientific, compassionate, and progressive. But peel back the surface, and you'll find something far more disturbing.

What if the aim of these medications is not healing, but *conformity*?

What if the purpose isn't to liberate the mind, but to tame it?

What if your consent to medicate was never truly informed, but manufactured through social pressure, fear, and systemic negligence?

This is the premise of chemical consent, not the conscious choice to heal, but the passive surrender to a system that defines dysfunction not by suffering, but by **non-compliance**.

A Personal Reckoning

I know this story intimately. I've lived it. I've swallowed the pills. I've endured the side effects. I've wrestled with the crushing internal silence they induced, not a quiet mind, but a muted soul.

The medications did not support my healing. They disconnected me from myself. Numbed me. Isolated me. Made me question my intuition and capacity. I wasn't getting healthier. I was becoming more manageable.

This isn't to say that no one benefits from psychiatric medication. Some do. But the broad and lazy application of such treatments, without deeply understanding the root of emotional distress, is not care. It's compliance enforcement.

Psychiatry or Social Control?

French philosopher Michel Foucault once described psychiatry as a tool of social discipline, a way for society to pathologise difference. In other words, those who think, feel, or behave outside the prescribed norms are labelled as ill, and their experiences are sanitised with medical language and subdued through pharmaceuticals.

Modern mental health systems operate within this logic. The DSM (Diagnostic and Statistical Manual of Mental Disorders) grows larger each decade, expanding the scope of what constitutes mental "illness," while the solutions remain curiously narrow: diagnose, label, medicate.

The complexity of human emotion is flattened into checklists. Grief becomes a disorder. Emotional sensitivity becomes a pathology. Spiritual awakening is repackaged as mania.

And once labelled, your fate is often sealed: a prescription pad, a treatment plan, and a subtle erasure of your inner wisdom.

The Systemic Setup

During my time working with the NHS, I witnessed this firsthand. Patients were processed. Emotional histories were glossed over in favour of pharmacological solutions. If they responded poorly to medication, the answer was often another pill, not a reassessment of the approach.

The root causes of suffering, trauma, abuse, alienation, and disconnection were rarely addressed in depth. Therapy was rationed. Time was limited. And the unspoken message was clear:

"You are broken. Take this. Get back to work."

That isn't mental health. It's emotional suppression. It's system-serving sedation.

Spiritual Symptoms, Misread

In 2017, I experienced a profound spiritual awakening. It shattered my worldview, opened my heart, and destabilised everything I thought I understood. It was raw, disorienting, and overwhelming, but it was not illness. It was growth.

Yet through the lens of psychiatry, such experiences are often misdiagnosed. Euphoric states become hypomania. Existential crises become disorders. Visions become hallucinations.

Carl Jung once warned of the "spiritual emergency", a process where awakening is mistaken for breakdown. If mishandled, the person can be traumatised by the very system that claims to help them.

And many are.

Informed Dissent

Years ago, I chose to stop taking psychiatric medications (disclaimer, this is not a suggestion for you to quit taking your medications) - I wanted to understand what was truly happening inside me, not suppress it. I adjusted my diet. I committed to deep introspection, physical exercise, somatic practices, and emotional regulation. It wasn't easy, but it was *mine*. It was real. And it worked.

The path to wholeness cannot be prescribed in 10-minute consultations. It must include the whole human body, mind, soul, environment, history, and purpose.

That's the real medicine.

The Choice to Heal

Healing is not compliance. It is not sedating discomfort. It is not flattening the edges of your emotions so you can perform in a sick society.

Healing is remembrance. Integration. Growth. And most of all, *choice*.

Your mind is not a machine with broken parts. Your emotions are not errors in the system. They are signals, asking to be felt, heard, and honoured.

Let us no longer consent to chemical shortcuts disguised as care. Let us choose to face ourselves, fully, courageously, and consciously.

Because you deserve more than sedation. You deserve transformation.

20

Integration Activity: Rethinking Support

If you've been diagnosed, medicated, or labelled:

1. Reflect on how the process felt. Did you feel seen, heard, and understood? Or were you processed?

2. Consider journaling about your experiences with emotional intensity.
   What did those feelings *want* from you?

3. Explore alternative frameworks:

   - Gabor Maté on trauma
   - Bessel van der Kolk on the body keeping the score
   - Jungian or transpersonal approaches to mental health
   - Somatic experiencing and breathwork

Use This Space To Make Notes

Part II: The Layers of Illusion

Diving into the structural illusions of modern life, morality, freedom, surveillance, and self-perception.

5. **Inverted Light — Good, Evil & the Myth of Moral Clarity**
   Questioning binary morality, virtue signalling, and the weaponisation of 'goodness.'

6. **The Consent Illusion — Freedom, Free Will & Invisible Coercion**
   The illusion of choice in a world of psychological nudges and manipulated decisions.

7. **Spectacle & Surveillance — The Theatre of Control**
   The panopticon of modern life: media theatrics, virtue optics, digital tracking, and self-censorship.

8. **Broken Mirrors — Identity Fragmentation in the Age of Hyperrealism**
   Dissociation, simulation, post-truth culture, and the fracturing of the unified self.

Use This Space To Make Notes

Chapter 5: Inverted Light — Good, Evil & the Myth of Moral Clarity

A World Upside Down

What if good wasn't good?

What if evil didn't wear horns, but a suit?

The world we live in doesn't suffer from a lack of morality. It suffers from **too much certainty** about morality. People don't question their side, only the other. The villain is always someone else. Never us.

This is the myth of moral clarity, the belief that good and evil are obvious, self-evident, neatly separated. But real life doesn't operate in binary. The most dangerous ideologies are not evil in appearance; they are *righteous*. They are built on the premise that they are saving you, helping you, and healing you. Until they're not.

Moral Inversion & Language Games

Many of the world's darkest moments were justified through twisted virtue:

- Wars framed as liberation.
- Censorship is framed as protection.
- Control framed as care.

George Orwell called this *doublethink*, the ability to hold two contradictory beliefs and accept both as true. Modern propaganda doesn't just lie. It flips the script. It inverts light into darkness and darkness into light.

Manufactured Consent

When people believe they are doing good, they become easier to control. This is why so many atrocities happen with public approval. The masses don't need to be evil, just misled. If the media says it's for the greater good, many comply. If the state says it's for safety, few resist. This is not to shame, it's to reveal how deep the programming runs. When you've been taught that obedience is moral, questioning becomes rebellion.

But rebellion is not inherently immoral. Sometimes it's the highest form of morality.

The Shadow of Righteousness

Carl Jung said, "The brighter the light, the darker the shadow."

Those who claim moral perfection cast the deepest shadows. The more someone speaks of saving the world, the more carefully you should watch their actions. The saviour archetype is powerful and often weaponised.

This is why many people who speak of unity, healing, and progress also engage in exclusion, judgment, and authoritarianism. The language is light. The actions are inverted.

Discernment Over Dogma

Real moral clarity requires **discernment**, not doctrine.

It means:

- Questioning your side.
- Listening to uncomfortable truths.
- Accepting that being wrong is part of growth.

True morality is less about declaring yourself right and more about living in integrity. It isn't loud. It isn't always popular. And it doesn't need applause.

Walking the Middle Path

You don't have to pick a side in every battle. You don't have to condemn or convert. You can choose the middle path, the path of understanding.

That doesn't mean neutrality in the face of injustice. It means clarity without dogma. Compassion without submission. Wisdom without pride.

To navigate this inverted world, you must learn to see through both the light and the shadow. Because often, what looks like salvation is just a prettier form of submission.

Integration Activity: Spot the Inversion

Choose a news headline, social movement, or public figure.

Ask yourself:

- What values are being expressed?
- Do the actions match the message?
- What might be the shadow beneath the light?

This exercise isn't about becoming cynical; it's about becoming conscious.

Use This Space To Make Notes

Chapter 6: The Consent Illusion — Freedom, Free Will & Invisible Coercion

The Illusion of Choice

We're told we're free. Free to speak. Free to think. Free to choose.

But how free are we when every option presented is already pre-selected, pre-approved, and pre-framed? Like a child offered the choice between broccoli and carrots, the meal is decided. You just get to pick the flavour of obedience.

Freedom in modern society often operates as an illusion: the illusion of consent. We say yes, not because we agree, but because the alternative is invisible, unspoken, or punished.

Coercion in Plain Sight

Real coercion isn't always violent. It doesn't need to be. The most effective control systems are subtle. They operate through:

- Social pressure
- Financial dependency
- Emotional manipulation
- Cultural expectation

You aren't told what to do. You're nudged. Suggested. Informed of consequences. Your "free" choices are made under duress, fear, or false urgency.

Framing the Narrative

Think about how questions are asked:

- "Do you want to protect your family by taking this injection?"
- "Will you comply with safety procedures or put others at risk?"

Both are coercive frames. The question assumes a moral position, then punishes any disagreement with guilt, shame, or exclusion.

This isn't education. It's manipulation.

Manufactured Desires

Many of our desires are not organic. They are manufactured through advertising, media, and peer reinforcement. We want what we're told to want. We chase dreams sold to us as success.

Even rebellion is often commodified. They sell you t-shirts with slogans about freedom while tracking your every move through your phone.

Free Will vs. Conditioned Will

True free will is difficult. It requires awareness of:

- Your conditioning
- Your trauma
- Your fears
- Your internalised scripts

Most people are acting from **conditioned will,** automated responses shaped by past rewards and punishments. This doesn't make them weak. It makes them *human*. But waking up means recognising the difference.

The Consent You Never Gave

Did you consent to be watched? To be profiled? To have your data mined, your mind nudged, your emotions gamified?

Probably not. But you agreed. You clicked "Accept." Because what choice did you have?

This is the essence of the consent illusion: agreement under false conditions. It's not just in surveillance. It's in medicine. Law. Media. Relationships. Every power structure that claims legitimacy must be examined.

Reclaiming Sovereignty

Freedom is not comfort. It's not easy. It's not doing whatever you want. Freedom is a **conscious choice**. The ability to step back, observe, and respond with integrity, not react from fear.

To reclaim your sovereignty:

- Question what you're told.
- Pause before you react.
- Say no when it matters.
- Say yes with full awareness.

You don't have to rebel against everything. Just stop giving your power away without noticing.

Integration Activity: Track a Choice

Over the next few days, track one decision you make each day. Ask:

- Did I choose this freely?
- What influenced me?
- What fears or rewards were present?

Then imagine how you might choose differently with full awareness. Practice that difference.

Use This Space To Make Notes

Chapter 7: Spectacle & Surveillance — The Theatre of Control

The Show Must Go On

We live in a theatre.

A spectacle so grand, so immersive, that most don't even realise they're watching a performance, or worse, playing a part.

From reality TV to presidential debates, from social justice outrage cycles to war coverage, society has been restructured into a performance of power. And like all theatre, it requires an audience. Eyes glued. Emotions manipulated. Attention monetised.

Guy Debord, in his seminal work *The Society of the Spectacle*, argued that modern life is no longer about being, but appearing. The real has been replaced by its representation. We are no longer governed by policy. We are governed by *perception*. It is not the truth that matters, but what *looks* like the truth. Not freedom, but what *feels* like freedom.

Surveillance: The Silent Director

The modern surveillance state doesn't just watch, it *directs*.

CCTV cameras, biometric databases, smart cities, AI-driven sentiment analysis, predictive policing. These are not isolated tools. They are nodes in an all-seeing network that reshapes behaviour through observation.

The chilling effect is real: people change their actions when they know they're being watched. What begins as observation becomes modification. What begins as safety becomes submission.

It's no longer necessary to violently control a population. You only need to convince them that they might be watched. The camera becomes the conscience.

Consent in the Age of Opt-Out

We're told we have a choice. But choice without clarity is coercion.

When every app asks for your data, when every device listens, when every policy is hidden behind fifty pages of legalese, *opting in* becomes the default. You don't consent. You comply passively, unknowingly.

This is the new contract: visibility in exchange for functionality. Privacy in exchange for convenience. We click "accept" not because we agree, but because there's no real alternative.

And still, we perform.

The Spectacle of Outrage & Obedience

Every few weeks, a new spectacle emerges. A scandal. A villain. A polarising event. People rush to take sides, to signal virtue, to be on the right side of history. Outrage becomes a form of participation. Hashtags become a moral alignment.

But here's the trick: While you're arguing over the latest social issue, legislation is passed in silence. Surveillance expands. Freedoms shrink. Rights erode.

The spectacle keeps you busy. Distracted. Activated, but not empowered.

Performative Dissent

Even rebellion has been commodified.

The system is clever. It sells you the appearance of resistance. Corporate slogans about empowerment. Products wrapped in activist language. "Authenticity" as a branding strategy.

You think you're fighting the machine while feeding it clicks, data, engagement, and money.

And when dissent does appear in raw, unfiltered form? It is shadowbanned. Demonetised. Deplatformed. Or worse, it's turned into content and sold back to you in diluted form.

The Exit Isn't Loud

Escaping the theatre doesn't require a spotlight. It doesn't require a dramatic monologue.

It requires subtlety. Quiet rebellion. Refusal to perform.

- You don't have to share every opinion.
- You don't have to react to every provocation.
- You don't have to attend every performance.

The real revolution is presence. Discernment. Living with intention rather than reaction. The actors will keep acting. The cameras will keep rolling. The spectacle will continue. But you can choose to step off stage.

Integration Activity: Surveillance Reflection

Spend one day observing how your behaviour changes when you believe you're being watched, online or offline.

Then ask:

- What am I censoring in myself?
- Who taught me to do that?
- What would it feel like to act without the audience?

Use This Space To Make Notes

Chapter 8: Broken Mirrors — Identity Fragmentation in the Age of Hyperrealism

The Splintered Self

Once upon a time, identity was rooted in community, family, trade, and place. You were a butcher, a son, a neighbour, a friend. There was still pressure, of course, but there was also cohesion, a centre that held.

Today, identity is modular. Liquid. Commodified. Performed. The internet promised connection but delivered an identity crisis. Social media didn't just offer you a window into others' lives; it handed you a thousand mirrors, all warped. And every day, you're forced to perform in front of them.

Hyperreality: The Copy Becomes the Truth

French theorist Jean Baudrillard warned of a world where representations replace reality. Where symbols become more real than what they refer to. He called this *hyperreality*.

In a hyperreal world:

- A selfie becomes more important than the moment itself.
- The online persona overshadows the inner life.
- The performance becomes the identity.

We live not to experience, but to document. Not to feel, but to share. Not to be, but to appear.

The Infinite Self vs. The Branded Self

You are a multi-dimensional being, capable of contradiction, growth, and complexity.

But platforms demand clarity. Algorithms reward consistency. People want you to be one thing, forever. So you shrink. You choose a role. You build a brand.

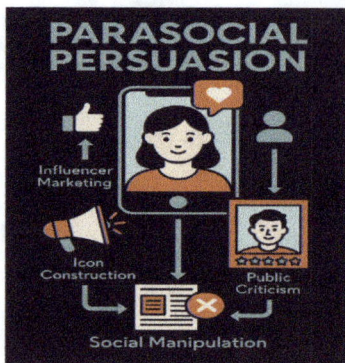

- The spiritual guy
- The activist
- The artist
- The mental health advocate

All are masks. Useful sometimes. But dangerous when fused with identity.

Fragmentation begins when we live too long in the mask and forget the face underneath.

Digital Schizophrenia

There is a kind of psychological dissociation that comes from switching roles so often:

- Professional at work.
- Sarcastic joker in group chats.
- Empathetic listener with friends.
- Filtered icon on social media.

Each role serves a purpose. But without grounding, we become emotionally disjointed, unsure of who we are without the screen, the affirmation, or the likes.

This is digital schizophrenia: a splitting of the self across platforms and contexts, until no unified self remains.

The Feedback Loop of Fragmentation

The more fragmented we feel, the more we seek validation. The more we seek validation, the more we perform. The more we perform, the less authentic we feel. And so it loops.

We become avatars of ourselves. Not only to others, but to our sense of self.

Realignment: From Persona to Presence

Healing the fractured self isn't about deleting social media or moving off-grid. It's about integration.

- Can you be consistent across spaces?
- Can you tell the truth without seeking applause?
- Can you honour your complexity without performing it?

Presence means showing up fully, not edited, not optimised, not polished. It means knowing that *who you are* can never be fully captured in a post or a persona.

Remembering Wholeness

You are not your brand. You are not your mistakes. You are not the filtered image or the clever post or the role you play to keep the peace.

You are a whole, living, breathing human, fragmented not by design, but by survival in a disjointed world.

To be whole again, don't seek perfection. Seek coherence. Find the through-line in your many selves. Let your masks fall where they may.

Because the real you, the unbroken mirror, was never truly gone. Just buried beneath the noise.

Integration Activity: Avatar Audit

- List all the versions of yourself you present in different areas of life.
- Reflect on how each version serves you, or hinders you.
- Choose one space this week to show up with more honesty.

Practice coherence. One choice at a time.

Use This Space To Make Notes

Part III: Remembering the Self

A return to the centre. Healing, reintegration, authenticity, and forward movement.

9. **Echoes of the Inner Child — Trauma, Repression & Emotional Memory**
Revisiting childhood wounds, family dynamics, and the echoes that shape adult life.

10. **Sovereign Signals — Intuition, Discernment & the Path to Wholeness**
Reclaiming inner guidance, letting go of the programmed identity, and rebuilding authenticity.

Use This Space To Make Notes

Chapter 9: Echoes of the Inner Child — Trauma, Repression & Emotional Memory

The Invisible Child Within

Every adult carries a child within them. Not in metaphor, but in neurological, emotional, and psychological reality. The "inner child" is not some abstract spiritual notion; it is the sum of your formative memories, beliefs, emotional blueprints, and unmet needs. And when trauma has occurred, especially when unacknowledged, that inner child speaks loudly, through silence, avoidance, emotional outbursts, dissociation, and patterns we can't quite explain.

I lived much of my life not fully understanding why I reacted the way I did, why moments of intense emotion would shut down my ability to speak rationally, or why I felt sadness and loneliness in cycles. Only through deep introspection, education, and self-examination did I realise: I had been dissociating since childhood. I had built up layers of emotional armour, not because I was broken, but because my environment hadn't felt fully safe.

There were times I just wanted to be alone. My body would ache. I would disconnect. I was misunderstood. I was seen as sensitive, overemotional, or even a problem, not out of malice, but because those around me didn't know how to deal with what they couldn't see. And so I buried those parts of myself. I survived. But I didn't thrive. Not yet.

Childhood Wounds, Adult Reactions

Unresolved childhood trauma doesn't vanish with age. It mutates. It resurfaces in subtle, insidious ways: trust issues, attachment struggles, people-pleasing, rage, or a need for constant validation. We see the world through the lens of wounds we haven't healed. We project, protect, and perform, often unconsciously, to defend the vulnerable child inside us who still longs to be heard, loved, and seen.

In relationships, I often found myself being misunderstood, even attacked for the very qualities that came from a place of love and concern. When I stood firm, I was labelled controlling. When I walked away, I was told I didn't care. The reality? I was finally learning to enforce boundaries. And not everyone welcomes the healing of someone they once controlled.

It took me a long time to understand that much of the pain I carried wasn't mine to begin with. It had been handed down. Projected onto me. I was carrying the pain of generations, parents doing their best, family members with unresolved trauma of their own, teachers who misread my sensitivity as defiance, friends who mirrored their wounds back at me. And in the midst of it all, I blamed myself.

But trauma isn't your fault. Healing, however, is your responsibility.

Dissociation: The Survival Strategy

Dissociation is not weakness. It's intelligence. It's your brain's way of protecting you from an overload of emotion, from an environment that felt unsafe or overwhelming. I now understand that what I experienced wasn't a personality flaw; it was a survival mechanism. And survival mechanisms become subconscious habits. We don't even notice when they run the show.

I would freeze. Go quiet. Struggle to articulate myself. I couldn't access my logical brain during heightened emotional states, and now I know why. Fight, flight, freeze or fawn. These aren't just responses; they are embedded physiological programs.

Children who experience neglect, inconsistency, or emotional invalidation learn to suppress their truth. Not because they are dishonest, but because their honesty wasn't welcomed. They learn to adapt. And those adaptations stay with us, hidden in adult behaviours that don't make sense until we trace them back.

The Repetition Compulsion

Psychoanalyst Sigmund Freud coined the term *repetition compulsion*, the tendency to repeat patterns of trauma in adult life in an attempt to gain mastery over them. We are drawn to familiar pain because it offers the illusion of control. We try to fix in adulthood what hurt us in childhood.

This is why so many trauma survivors end up in cycles of unhealthy relationships, careers that burn them out, or self-sabotaging behaviour. It's not that we are broken. It's that our nervous system is still trying to resolve what it never got to complete.

Recognising this changes everything. It means we are not victims of our past; we are witnesses to it. And that awareness can become the first tool of transformation.

Healing Through Awareness

Healing isn't linear. It's messy, circular, and at times deeply painful. But it is possible. And it begins with awareness. When I began to trace the roots of my emotional responses, I stopped demonising them. I stopped fighting myself. I stopped blaming the world. I began listening. Genuinely listening to my body, my memories, my intuition.

I revisited my childhood through the eyes of compassion, not critique. I gave my younger self the validation he never received. I stopped trying to be strong all the time. I allowed myself to grieve, not just events, but the love, clarity, and understanding I didn't receive. I realised that healing wasn't about going back and changing the past. It was about *re-parenting* myself in the present.

No therapist, book, or guide can do that part for you. But they can help you remember: you are not alone.

Integration Activity: Meet the Inner Child

Find a quiet space. Close your eyes. Imagine your younger self, at whatever age the pain seems to originate from. What does that version of you look like? What are they feeling? What do they need to hear?

Now, speak to them. Out loud or silently. Reassure them. Hold them in your heart.

Then ask:

- What have I been carrying that no longer belongs to me?
- What would my inner child thank me for doing today?
- How can I honour their truth moving forward?

You'll be amazed at what comes through.

Use This Space To Make Notes

Chapter 10: Sovereign Signals — Intuition, Discernment & the Path to Wholeness

Beyond the Noise: Tuning Into Inner Truth

In a world overflowing with advice, opinions, algorithms, and unsolicited input, the greatest act of rebellion might be this: to trust yourself.

Not your trauma. Not your ego. Not your learned responses. But the deepest part of you, the quiet, unwavering core that has always been present, even when life's chaos tried to drown it out. That part is your intuition. And it's not a fantasy. It's your most natural intelligence.

For a long time, I couldn't hear it. My intuition had been muted, fogged by medication, suppressed by social pressure, interrupted by emotional overwhelm. I second-guessed myself. I gave too much of my energy to people who didn't respect it. I abandoned my inner knowing to fit into systems that didn't see me.

But slowly, through discipline, solitude, and reflection, I started to notice the signal through the noise. I stopped giving out energy freely. I observed. I listened to myself and others. I slowed down. I chose who I gave my time and truth to. And my inner clarity returned.

Intuition Is Not a Feeling — It's a Signal

Intuition isn't just a gut feeling. It's a physiological, somatic signal, a neural response that bypasses the conscious mind and speaks through the body. It is not irrational. It is pre-rational. A knowing before knowing. A map your nervous system draws before your logic catches up.

Many of us have been taught to ignore it. Conditioned to distrust ourselves. The school system tells us there's one correct answer. The workplace demands compliance. Institutions reward deference, not discernment. And so, we become unsure. Disconnected. Dependent on external validation.

But the more we disconnect from our intuition, the more susceptible we become to manipulation. The inability to discern truth from illusion is not a failure of intelligence; it's a side effect of emotional disempowerment.

The Role of Discernment

Discernment is not judgment. It's not cynicism. It's the ability to hold space for possibility while still applying reason. It's the mature cousin of intuition, a balanced evaluation that doesn't rely on fear or ego.

Discernment is what allows you to hear a charismatic speaker and not be seduced. To see beyond the façade of political performance. To feel when something is "off", even if it looks good on paper. It is what keeps you sovereign in a world built on influence.

In my journey, I noticed that the more I discerned clearly, the more I was labelled as difficult or uncooperative. But that didn't bother me. Because discernment is not about pleasing others, it's about remaining in integrity with yourself.

Ego Death & the Return to Self

Part of reconnecting to intuition and discernment involves a process many call ego death. That term gets thrown around carelessly, but for me, it was real.

I had to dismantle the identity I built to survive, the people-pleaser, the overachiever, the reactive child. I had to accept that many of my actions were shaped by fear of abandonment, the need to be heard, and the pain of being misunderstood. I wasn't wrong for feeling those things. But I could no longer let them guide me.

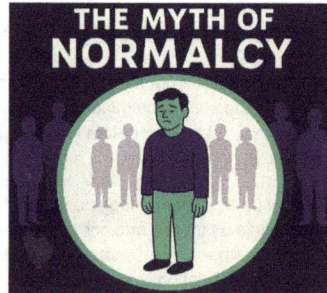

THE MYTH OF NORMALCY

The ego is not evil. It's a tool. But when we're ruled by it, we mistake protection for personality. True sovereignty means recognising when your ego is defending a wound, and choosing not to let it lead. I no longer argue to be right. I don't speak to be seen.

I speak when it serves clarity. I move when it aligns with my purpose. I live slower, deeper, and more intentionally, not because I've become passive, but because I've reclaimed agency over my pace and my path.

The Compass of Wholeness

The journey of this book, and life, is not to become perfect. It is to become whole.

Wholeness is not the absence of pain. It is the ability to contain contradictions without being torn apart. It is knowing that you can feel doubt and still move forward. That you can be uncertain and still grounded. That you can trust yourself, even if others don't.

Intuition and discernment are not separate from reason. They are its foundation. When you reconnect to them, the world no longer feels like a fog of endless options. It becomes navigable. Not easy. But honest. And in a dishonest world, honesty is a revolutionary act.

Integration Activity: Building Sovereignty

Over the next few days, practice pausing before making any decision, big or small. Ask:

- What is my first inner signal?
- Am I reacting from fear or responding from clarity?
- If no one had an opinion, what would I choose?

The goal is not perfection; it's to rebuild trust with your inner guidance system.

Use This Space To Make Notes

Part IV: Consciousness, Code & Culture

The metaphysical horizon. Questioning the nature of reality, language, and the symbolic systems that script our world.

11. The Myth of Sanity — Madness, Genius & the Edge of Perception
Reframing the boundaries between mental illness, creativity, and spiritual insight.

12. Simulated Souls — Reality, Illusion & the Code of Consciousness
Are we living in a simulation? This chapter delves into the symbolic architecture of reality,

13. Belief Machines — Language, Desire & the Engine of Reality
Language is a spell

Use This Space To Make Notes

Chapter 11: The Myth of Sanity — Madness, Genius & the Edge of Perception

Sanity: A Social Construct?

Who decides what is sane? What behaviours are acceptable? What thoughts are rational?

Sanity has never been a fixed truth. It is defined by cultural norms, medical consensus, and, too often, political convenience. In some cultures, hearing voices is divine. In others, it's pathology. In some eras, non-conformity is genius. In others, it's heresy.

The line between madness and brilliance is not only thin, it is shifting.

Neurodivergence: Gifts and Ghosts

I was diagnosed with Autism, ADHD, and Bipolar Type II. Each of these labels brought me pain and liberation. Pain because they carried stigma, misunderstanding, and limitation. Liberation, because they finally gave shape to my lifelong struggle.

But here's the thing: I am not my diagnosis. I am a complex human being with a unique pattern of perception, thought, and feeling. For much of my life, I was made to feel broken for that. But what if our differences aren't deficiencies? What if they are adaptations to a world out of balance?

The Genius of Altered States

Many of history's greatest minds would today be medicated into submission. Visionaries, mystics, scientists, and artists, all touched by a madness that allowed them to see the world differently. To peer beyond the veil. Altered states of consciousness, be they through suffering, meditation, psychedelics, or psychosis, have often revealed deep truths about reality, self, and society. Yet our system treats these states with fear, not reverence.

What we call a breakdown may often be the **start** of a breakthrough.

The Trauma Behind the "Crazy"

Labelling someone insane is often a way of silencing them. It makes their words ignorable. Their insights are dismissible. But madness can be a language of pain, of resistance, of transformation.

People fragment under pressure. They dissociate to survive. They experience heightened sensitivity as a way to navigate emotional chaos. This isn't always a disorder. Sometimes, it's a highly intelligent, albeit misunderstood, adaptation.

We must stop asking "what's wrong with you" and start asking:

"What happened to you?"

Madness in a Mad World

To be well-adjusted to a sick society is not a virtue. Often, it is the truly *sane* who feel the most distressed. Because they feel everything. Because they see what others deny. Because they refuse to numb themselves.

And so we must ask: If our world is fragmented, is it madness to shatter? Or is it a rational response to an irrational structure?

The Return to Wholeness

True sanity isn't about performing normalcy. It's about integrating the fragmented self, welcoming all parts of our psyche: the wounded child, the ecstatic visionary, the raging protector, the grieving soul.

Madness often invites us to **feel** what society tells us to hide. To collapse the masks. To confront the self. And if held properly, with care, not control, it can be the catalyst for radical transformation.

What we call "healing" is not returning to how we were. It's becoming who we are.

Integration Activity: Embrace the Misfit

- Think of a time you were called "too much" or "not enough."
- Reflect: Was it because you violated a cultural script? Or expressed something others feared?
- Write a letter to that version of yourself, not to correct it, but to honour it.

Sometimes, the parts we're most ashamed of are the ones closest to our truth.

Use This Space To Make Notes

Chapter 12: Simulated Souls & Manufactured Realities

Welcome to the Hyperreal

There is a difference between reality and representation. A tree is real. A photograph of a tree is a representation. But what happens when the photograph becomes more meaningful to people than the tree itself?

That's the world we now live in, the *hyperreal*. A world where simulations replace direct experience. Where social media personas carry more weight than lived integrity. We've become avatars of ourselves, performing curated identities inside a global digital theatre.

Jean Baudrillard, the philosopher who coined the term "hyperreality," argued that modern life is increasingly dominated by simulations: signs and images that no longer refer to anything real. We no longer chase truth; we chase the most persuasive illusion.

And the danger isn't just that we're being fooled. It's that we *prefer* the illusion.

Predictive Programming & the Control of Expectation

Have you ever watched a dystopian film, only to see its themes manifest in real life years later? It's not a coincidence. It's predictive programming: the use of fiction and entertainment to subtly acclimate the public to future societal changes.

When I first started noticing this, I thought I was being paranoid. But again and again, I saw the same pattern. The technologies, crises, policies, and even language of the future were being rehearsed in our collective imagination long before they arrived. Films like *Contagion*, *Minority Report*, *The Matrix*, or *Black Mirror* became less entertainment, more instruction manuals. This isn't prophecy. It's preparation. These stories shape our expectations and normalise the absurd. When it arrives, we're not shocked. We're already scripted.

AI Avatars & Digital Possession

We used to ask: *Who are you?* Now we ask: *What's your handle?*

The rise of artificial intelligence and digital avatars has blurred the lines between real people and synthetic personas. Filters, voice modulation, ChatGPT-written bios, AI-generated influencers, we are entering a reality where the self is endlessly edited, optimised, and eventually… replaced.

What does this do to the soul? When you no longer recognise your voice, your face, your intuition, have you not become digitally possessed?

Identity in the digital age is not discovered. It's *manufactured*. And the more we conform to platform aesthetics and algorithmic reward systems, the more we trade authenticity for relevance. It's not just about technology. It's about spiritual erosion.

Dopamine Loops & the Hijack of Attention

Attention is currency. Every second you spend online is monetised, tracked, and sold. The architects of digital space know this, and they engineer platforms accordingly: infinite scroll, red notifications, variable reward systems, the exact mechanisms used in casinos.

It's not accidental that we feel addicted. It's not a side effect. It's the *design*.

And what is lost in the process? Deep thought. Stillness. Boredom. Presence. Genuine connection. We've traded our inner worlds for feedback loops.

When the Fake Becomes Realer Than Real

The hyperreal doesn't just simulate life. It competes with it. A celebrity scandal feels more real to some than their family dynamics. A livestreamed war seems more important than the quiet conflicts in their own home. A tweet feels more urgent than an inner voice.

Simulated souls are the result: people whose emotions, desires, and identities are shaped more by external signals than internal reflection.

I experienced this too. I had moments where I lost track of who I was, where I began to perform even my healing process. I noticed how easy it is to become a symbol, a brand, an idea, instead of a living, evolving human being. It's intoxicating. But ultimately, it's a trap.

Reclaiming the Real

Escaping the hyperreal doesn't require full withdrawal. It requires awareness. Boundaries. Stillness. The courage to be invisible again. To feel the breeze, unfiltered. To experience pain, unsedated. To speak without audience approval. To reconnect with what's *real*, not because it performs well, but because it nourishes.

The soul cannot thrive in simulation. It only lives in present. In truth. In silence. In stillness. If we are to heal, individually and collectively, we must remember:

We were not born to be content. We were born to be conscious.

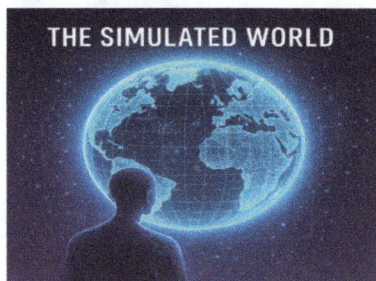

Integration Activity: Digital Fast & Presence Audit

- Take one full day without digital interaction. No phone. No social media. No screens.
- During this time, notice how often your mind seeks stimulation. Notice any discomfort.
- Write down any emotions, ideas, or memories that surface.

Then ask:

- What parts of myself have I outsourced to machines?
- What does my body, not my feed, say I need?

Use This Space To Make Notes

Chapter 13: Belief Machines — Language, Desire & the Engine of Reality

The Spell of Language

Language is not neutral. It is not merely a way to describe reality; it shapes it. It encodes belief systems, frames perception, and steers emotional responses. When you speak, you cast spells. When you repeat phrases passed down by culture or authority, you invoke inherited assumptions. Most of us don't realise we are under these spells because they've been normalised into everyday conversation.

Think of phrases like:

- "It's just the way things are."
- "You can't fight the system."
- "That's not realistic."

These aren't neutral expressions. They are encoded limits, invisible fences around what is considered acceptable, possible, or sane.

Memetics and Cultural Propagation

Memetics, the study of how ideas spread, reveals that thoughts behave like viruses. They propagate not because they are true, but because they are catchy. Media, advertising, politics, and even education systems are memetic battlegrounds, vying for your attention and allegiance. The idea isn't just to inform you, it's to *form you.*

Popular slogans, marketing jingles, and ideological catchphrases embed themselves deep in the psyche. From Nike's "Just Do It" to government campaigns like "Build Back Better," language is weaponised to manufacture consent, direct action, and prevent dissent. As George Orwell warned, the manipulation of language is the manipulation of thought.

Desire Engineering

Desire isn't natural. It's designed. What you crave, from romantic partners to tech gadgets to social validation, is often the result of prolonged psychological conditioning. The world tells you what to want. And in many cases, you obey, thinking those desires are your own.

Behind the curtain is a system engineered to capitalise on your dissatisfaction. You are sold identity, success, beauty, happiness, always just out of reach. This constant longing fuels economies and distracts from deeper questions. If you ever truly felt fulfilled, the system would collapse.

The Reality Engine

Belief is the fuel of reality. What you believe affects how you perceive, how you interpret events, how you emotionally respond, and what you think is possible. Change your beliefs, and your world shifts with them.

But beliefs aren't always conscious. Many are installed covertly:

- Through repetition
- Through emotionally charged stories
- Through shame and praise
- Through linguistic framing

You don't need chains to enslave people. You need only to convince them that their chains are natural. Or that they aren't wearing any at all.

Breaking the Machine

To break free from the belief machine, you must:

1. **Become linguistically sovereign** – Watch your words. Notice the hidden assumptions they carry.
2. **Interrogate your desires** – Ask: Who benefits from me wanting this? What am I compensating for?
3. **Observe the loop** – Catch the memetic scripts you've inherited. Stop reciting spells that harm you.
4. **Reclaim your imagination** – The system can predict your next thought. Surprise it.

There is no final truth offered in this chapter. Only a mirror. You are the spellcaster. The meaning-maker. The architect of your perception. This is not just a chapter — it is an incantation for liberation.

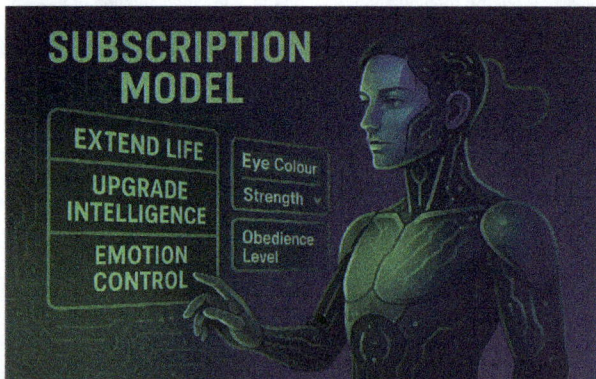

Integration Activity: Decode the Spell

Over the next week, observe how language influences your emotions and decisions. Each time you find yourself saying or thinking something familiar, pause. Ask:

- Who taught me to speak or think this way?
- What belief is embedded in this phrase?
- Is it empowering, limiting, or manipulative?

Then rewrite the sentence in a way that reflects your truth, not the script you inherited.

Use This Space To Make Notes

Part V: Tools for Conscious Living

Exploring deprogramming in action, this section offers a glossary of psychological and social control mechanisms, embodied awareness practices, symbolic decoding, and perception recovery tools. It empowers the reader to not only see through illusion but to live beyond it.

14. Decoding the Illusion — A Glossary of Influence & Identity

This glossary provides working definitions of key terms explored in *The Inversiverse*. These concepts form the hidden architecture of perception, behaviour, belief, and control. Interwoven with personal reflections and practical interpretation, this is not an academic list; it's a toolkit for decoding reality.

Use This Space To Make Notes

Chapter 14 - A Glossary of Influence & Identity

1. **Cognitive Dissonance** - *The psychological discomfort experienced when holding conflicting beliefs or values.*

   In a world layered with contradiction, dissonance is a clue, not a flaw. It's what I felt when I first questioned the mental health system. Discomfort meant awareness was knocking.

2. **Indoctrination** - *The process of conditioning individuals to accept a set of beliefs uncritically.*

   From school pledges to medical compliance, indoctrination hides beneath the banner of 'normal.' We refer to it as education or culture, but it often stifles independent thought.

Sometimes one illusion hides behind another. As we move through these terms, remember: this isn't just about understanding systems, it's about revealing how we've internalised them. Every definition is an invitation to observe your conditioning.

3. **Mimetic Desire** - *The subconscious imitation of others' desires.*

   Much of what we want is learned by watching others. Mimetic loops shape trends, goals, even identities. Recognising this helped me deconstruct the career, relationships, and status I once pursued.

4. **False Consensus Effect** - *The tendency to overestimate how much others share our beliefs.*

   It's easy to assume our perspective is widely held, especially when media and algorithms reinforce it. But the truth isn't found in volume, it's found in clarity.

5. **Confirmation Bias** - *The tendency to search for and interpret information in a way that confirms existing beliefs.*

   I once read articles only to validate my views. Now I ask: does this challenge me? Bias isn't weakness, it's default. Awareness turns it into strength.

6. **Gaslighting** - *A manipulation tactic to make someone doubt their reality or sanity.*

   Gaslighting isn't just interpersonal. Entire systems do it. Diagnoses, labels, and social narratives can all distort your perception of yourself.

7. **Normalcy Bias** - *The refusal to plan for or react to disasters that haven't happened before.*

   Societies ignore danger signs because "it hasn't happened yet." I ignored internal alarms until breakdown forced me to re-evaluate everything.

8. **Inversion** - *The flipping of truth and lie, health and sickness, freedom and control.*

   The Inversiverse itself is built on inversion, where what is sold as light may be darkness, and what is labelled madness may be insight.

9. **Identity Performance** - *The curated display of self to meet social expectations.*

   For years, I wore masks to appear "functional." Masking wasn't just social, it was spiritual. I performed safety while silently unravelling.

The deeper you look, the more these mechanisms connect. Each one touches another bias, fuels consensus, consensus fuels performance, performance feeds repression. Awareness doesn't isolate, it integrates.

10. **Neurodivergence** - *The natural variation in cognitive processing, perception, and behaviour.*

    Being autistic didn't make me broken; it made me perceptive. The pain came from trying to contort myself into neurotypical moulds.

11. **Symbolic Reality** - *The layer of meaning constructed through language, symbols, and media.*

    We live inside a story, not just a system. Words shape belief. Narratives shape memory. Whoever controls the symbols controls perception.

12. **Subconscious Programming** - *The installation of behavioural patterns outside conscious awareness.*

    Repetition, trauma, and suggestion embed scripts within us. Deprogramming is slow but possible. It starts with naming what no longer serves.

13. **Trauma Looping** - *The repeated reactivation of unresolved emotional wounds.*

    Until I faced the root, I kept reenacting the same emotional patterns in different contexts. Reflection broke the loop. Awareness is the exit.

14. **Emotional Repression** - *The suppression of feelings deemed unsafe, inconvenient, or irrational.*

    Most of us were trained to hide emotion. But repressed emotion doesn't disappear; it festers, distorts, and eventually erupts.

15. **Inner Child** - *The emotionally imprinted self that developed in early life.*

    This child is not weak. It's the keeper of truth, innocence, and unmet needs. Listening to them is how we reparent ourselves into wholeness.

16. **Thought-Terminating Cliché -** *A commonly used phrase that halts deeper questioning or critical thinking.*

   Phrases like "It is what it is" or "That's just the way things are" stop us from examining the system. Language can be a tool of liberation or sedation.

17. **Groupthink -** *The loss of individual perspective in favour of consensus within a group.*

   In the pursuit of harmony, dissent becomes taboo. I've watched intelligent people silence their insight to avoid friction. Collective delusion thrives in agreement.

18. **Social Scripts -** *Culturally assigned behavioural patterns that dictate how to act in specific roles.*

   These unspoken codes told me how to behave as a man, a patient, and a professional. The moment I questioned the script, I found the actor and the author.

19. **Mass Formation -** *A psychological state where individuals surrender autonomy to group identity under conditions of fear or uncertainty.*

   Mass formation turns complexity into slogans and nuance into heresy. We saw it unfold during global crises, where panic blurred moral lines.

By now, you may recognise these aren't just definitions, they're lenses. Change the lens, and reality shifts. You're not collecting terms. You're assembling a mirror.

20. **Ideological Possession -** *When beliefs control a person, rather than being tools of understanding.*

   I've been there, where the idea becomes your identity. To let go feels like death, but it's rebirth. Ideas are lenses, not cages.

21. **Liminality -** *A threshold state between identities, roles, or realities.*

   The in-between is uncomfortable, but it's also sacred. This is where transformation occurs, between illusion and insight, between stories.

22. **Emotional Contagion -** *The unconscious transfer of feelings and emotional states from others.*

   I often absorbed the moods of those around me without realising it. Learning to discern what was mine from what was ambient changed everything.

23. **Moral Panic -** *A wave of fear that a person or group threatens societal values, often fueled by media.*

   It's a distraction tactic, misdirecting anger toward symptoms rather than systems. The outrage machine thrives on scapegoats.

24. **Narrative Control -** *The shaping of public perception through selective storytelling and information management.*

   What we see, hear, and believe is often curated. Those who control the narrative control the consensus.

25. **Somatic Intelligence -** *The body's capacity to sense, signal, and respond to truth or misalignment.*

   Before the mind catches up, the body knows. My stomach churned before I could name a lie. Listening to my body brought me back to the truth.

Language opens the door. Awareness walks through it. But practice, that's where it becomes real. These terms are not meant to be memorised, but metabolised. They are not answers, but openings.

You've just walked through a hall of mirrors. Some were clean, some distorted. Some showed you society; others showed you. These concepts are not simply labels; they're keys to locked doors we never realised we were behind. But even keys need hands to turn them.

The real transformation begins when insight is lived, not just understood. The purpose of language is not only to define reality, but to reshape it. These terms gave you new eyes; now it's time to build new pathways.

The next section invites you to act, not just reflect, to bring the internal into the external, and the conscious into the everyday. You are not a passive observer in this world. You are a participant, a signal, a sovereign being.

So let's turn reflection into motion. Let's take the next step, deliberately, courageously, and awake.

Use This Space To Make Notes

Practices for Perception

Language as a Diagnostic Tool — Spotting Manipulation and the Dark Triad

These are not hacks. They are practices of awareness designed to gently undo illusion, stimulate internal clarity, and deepen sovereignty. Unlike productivity strategies or surface-level affirmations, these actions are rooted in research, lived experience, and long-observed psychospiritual insight.

The practices that follow draw not only from trauma-informed therapeutic models (van der Kolk, 2014; Siegel, 2012) and mindfulness-based stress reduction (Kabat-Zinn, 1990), but also from my journey of unmasking, deconstructing, and integrating. They serve as invitations to move from insight to embodiment. From theoretical clarity to lived authenticity.

The cost of staying masked is immense. We lose clarity, energy, and truth. We may be socially accepted, but spiritually starving. On the surface, masks keep us safe. But over time, they isolate us from the very parts of ourselves most capable of healing.

I know this personally. The years I spent performing professionalism while suppressing my autistic sensitivity led to exhaustion, panic, and numbness. Only by slowly integrating honest reflection, emotional expression, and body awareness did I begin to restore a sense of internal coherence.

Each practice below is chosen for its simplicity and psychological grounding, yet its power lies in repetition and intention. These are tools for reprogramming perception, not bypassing pain.

1. **Daily Deconstruction**
   Each evening, write down three unquestioned assumptions you held that day. Ask: Where did they come from? Are they mine? This practice dismantles mental automation and strengthens discernment. It echoes the cognitive-behavioural technique of identifying core beliefs and reframing distorted thought patterns.

2. **Media Fasting**
   Once a week, spend 24 hours without news, social media, or content. Notice your emotional baseline. What emerges in the silence? Research shows media exposure increases cortisol, distorts empathy, and reduces sustained attention (Twenge et al., 2018). Silence is not absence; it is recalibration.

3. **Mirror Dialogue**
Speak aloud to yourself for five minutes in the mirror. Not affirmations, truths. Let your mask fall and observe what remains. This echoes Gestalt empty-chair work and somatic witnessing. When I first tried this, I cried within minutes. I had not spoken with honesty to myself in years.

4. **Inversion Tracing**
Choose a cultural "truth" and invert it. Explore what becomes visible. Example: "Productivity equals worth." Try its opposite: "Stillness reveals value." This opens up neuroplastic flexibility and unearths hidden scripts. Philosophers like Foucault and critical theorists like Adorno relied on this inversion lens to reveal power structures.

5. **Inner Child Letter**
Write to yourself at age 7. Then respond from that age. Read it aloud. This emotional dialogue builds integration across dissociated parts of the self. It's similar to Internal Family Systems (IFS) therapy, which has shown promising results in trauma resolution (Schwartz, 2019).

6. **Breath-Pattern Tracking**
Set a timer 3 times daily. When it rings, check your breath: is it shallow, held, hurried? The breath reflects the nervous system's regulation. By observing without changing it, you begin building interoceptive awareness, the first step in self-regulation.

7. **Symbol Disruption**
Find one logo, phrase, or icon you pass every day. Write about what it sells, what it hides, and how it programs perception. Symbolic awareness helps decode the media matrices we're embedded within.

8. **Silence Immersion**
Spend 30 minutes in complete silence. No phone, no music, no reading. Just you. Many people experience initial resistance or anxiety, proof that noise has become a comfort blanket. But in silence, the psyche surfaces. Jung wrote, "Who looks outside, dreams; who looks inside, awakens."

9. **Emotion Labeling**
When overwhelmed, pause and name your emotion using the sentence: "A part of me feels..." This aligns with both mindfulness and polyvagal theory, naming feelings shifts them from limbic chaos into prefrontal processing. It reduces shame and re-engages self-compassion.

10. **Exit the Room**
If a conversation, setting, or group feels misaligned, practice exiting with no explanation. This is not rude. It's sovereignty. When I began doing this, I lost shallow ties but gained integrity. Learning to walk away is part of learning to stay aligned.

Remember: you're not performing healing. You're returning to wholeness. These practices are not about becoming someone new. They're about remembering who you were before the conditioning took hold.

Just as we use reflective tools to realign with our authentic self, we must also sharpen our ability to detect manipulation, especially from individuals who operate from darker psychological patterns.

The Dark Triad, comprising narcissism, Machiavellianism, and psychopathy, is not merely a clinical categorisation; it's an archetypal map of how ego, control, and emotional detachment can hijack language and interaction.

Language reveals what masks conceal. Spotting manipulative intent often starts with recognising subtle linguistic cues. These include:

1. **Word Salad and Obfuscation**
   Dark Triad individuals often use convoluted or vague speech to destabilise clarity. In my past experiences with manipulative professionals, I noticed how they avoided direct answers and weaponised ambiguity. The tactic isn't just confusion, it's control.

2. **Conditional Empathy**
   Phrases like "I understand, but..." or "If you were smarter, you'd see..." feign empathy while undermining autonomy. Narcissistic communicators often sandwich invalidation between gestures of concern.

3. **Deflection and Projection**
   Machiavellian types rarely answer criticism directly. Instead, they reroute blame ("You're too sensitive") or shift focus ("Why are you making this about you?"). This is not dialogue, it's diversion.

4. **High-Fluency Deception**
   Psychopaths, especially in high-functioning forms, may use charm and rapid, fluid language to build trust quickly. This is what psychologists Paul Babiak and Robert Hare called "impression management." They aren't connecting, they're conditioning.

5. **Overuse of Absolutes**
   Statements like "Everyone agrees with me" or "You always do this" signal cognitive rigidity and pressure conformity. These absolutes discourage nuance, which is the natural habitat of critical thinking.

Analytical Techniques

Pattern Recognition
Review conversations over time. Are there recurring inconsistencies? Does the individual rewrite history, contradict themselves, or subtly reshape facts? Journaling conversations, as I did during my psychiatric work, revealed these manipulative patterns over time.

Pronoun Shifts
Listen for the use of "you" in conflict rather than "I." Manipulators externalise blame: "You made me angry," versus "I felt angry." This linguistic distancing is a defence mechanism and a red flag.

Silence and Response Time
How long do they pause before replying? Psychopaths tend to respond rapidly and fluently even to complex questions, showing rehearsed answers. In contrast, genuine empathy and reflection often create natural pauses.

Mirroring Detection
Charismatic manipulators use mirroring (copying your tone, posture, or values) to build false rapport. If you feel unusually "seen" early in an interaction, pause. Ask: Are they reflecting me or constructing a mask?

Psychological Effects and Stakes

Remaining unaware of these patterns can result in:

Chronic self-doubt and cognitive dissonance, Emotional exhaustion and decision paralysis and Erosion of boundaries and authentic expression. In contrast, learning to detect these patterns empowers you to:

Reclaim narrative authority, exit toxic dynamics early and cultivate resilience and discernment

My awakening to this came through a painful mentorship experience. I trusted charisma over character, rhetoric over reality. By the time I noticed the gaslighting and coercion, my sense of clarity had been deeply fractured. It took months of study and written deconstruction to restore my inner compass.

Practice: Conversational Autopsy

After any emotionally charged exchange, write a "conversation autopsy." What was said? What wasn't? Which words triggered reactivity? This builds linguistic intuition and reveals the subtle architecture of manipulation. Over time, this technique restored my confidence in perception and rebuilt internal coherence.

Language is not just a tool for communication; it's a diagnostic lens. Learn to listen for tone, tempo, tension, and truth. And remember: manipulation often wears the mask of charisma.

Discernment isn't paranoia. It's the boundary between sovereignty and submission.

Symbolic Map — Visual Anchors for Awakening

Symbols are the subconscious language of the mind. While words shape thought, symbols shape belief. Visuals bypass analytical resistance and speak directly to emotion, memory, and intuition. This section invites you to explore the symbolic landscape of perception through curated visuals, colour practices, reflective drawing, and the metaphysical function of creativity in healing and unmasking.

In traditional cultures, symbols were not mere artistic flourishes; they were instruments of knowledge transmission, behavioural shaping, and cosmological anchoring. In modernity, they are often hijacked by branding and commodification. But here, we reclaim them. We re-enter the symbolic dimension as a conscious act of meaning-making.

Image Reflections: Seeing the Self Through Symbol

Use the following thematic image prompts not only as contemplation tools but as portals into deeper layers of your unconscious. Rather than merely viewing them, interact with them. Annotate, redraw, colour, disrupt, invert.

Prompts:

- A marionette figure with strings labelled "approval," "achievement," and "identity" Which string is pulled most often in your life?

- A face divided in two, one half smiling, the other shadowed, framed in pixelation and static. What emotional truth is hidden beneath your performance?

- A maze labelled "NORMAL," with exits marked "Sovereignty," "Sanity," and "Self" Where are you in the maze?

- A mirror breaking into fragments, each piece containing a word like "truth," "illusion," or "self" Which shards are you still trying to hold together?

Visual prompts awaken intuition. They bypass defensiveness. They hold up a mirror not to how we think, but how we feel and embody our reality.

Create Here

Colour as Alchemy: Mindful Mark-Making

Adult symbolic colouring may seem trivial, but it is a deeply meditative, neuro-regulating act. Colouring demands presence. It reconnects cognitive focus with tactile embodiment. It encourages the nervous system to slow, soften, and observe.

Practice this ritual: Use the provided Inversiverse symbol outline. As you colour:

- Assign each section a memory, belief, or emotion
- Use colours as mood indicators or energetic states
- Let the pattern become a dialogue, not a task

For me, colouring became a subconscious diagnostic tool. The areas I rushed through often mirrored life zones I neglected. The ones I avoided altogether revealed internalised shame. By staying present with the discomfort, insight followed.

Why this matters: Studies have shown that mandala colouring, in particular, significantly reduces anxiety and enhances emotional processing (Curry & Kasser, 2005).

This isn't a distraction; it's slow integration.

Draw Your Inversiverse: Your Reality Map

This exercise asks you to reconstruct your cosmology, not with words, but with image, intuition, and metaphor.

Use a blank page or use the space provided to represent:

- The ideologies that shaped your early worldview (symbolise these as weather systems, constellations, buildings)

- The roles you were expected to play (render these as costumes, cages, or masks)

- The 'break' or awakening (use colour, fragmentation, or disruption)

- Your reclaimed or emerging identity (create a symbol that represents the new you)

What this reveals: Drawing your inner world makes abstract beliefs visible. It allows emotional distance from shame or confusion. This is not a test of skill, but of presence. The aim is not accuracy, but honesty.

Create Here

Metaphor Mapping: Translating Belief Into Image

Choose five core beliefs you currently hold, whether liberating or limiting. Now translate each into a visual metaphor. For example:

- "I must always help others", → an overgrown garden choking the house

- "My worth is based on achievement" → a ticking clock with legs

- "I am finally enough" → a seedling growing through concrete

This matters because: Metaphor is the language of the subconscious.

Cognitive therapy often stops at thought. Symbolic inquiry goes deeper. It reveals the architecture beneath.

When I mapped my belief, "I need to appear fine," I drew a theatre mask nailed to a tired face. I couldn't unsee it afterwards. The next time I defaulted to performance, the image surfaced.

That's how symbols work; they haunt us with truth until we change.

Create Here

Visual Anchoring for Key Concepts

Create small, visual reminders, anchor images, for the core themes of this book. Place them in your journal, workspace, or meditation area.

Examples:

- Trauma Looping: a snake eating its tail

- Groupthink: a row of identical houses

- Narrative Control: a puppet master holding a book

- Subconscious Programming: a radio tower emitting spirals

- Discernment: a magnifying glass over a shadow

These images allow passive environments to become active allies. They tune perception. They serve as micro-interruptions to trance states.

Create Here

Visual Practices for Emotional Regulation

When verbal processing is overwhelming or inaccessible, visual expression becomes essential. Use drawing and colouring not to escape, but to decode and discharge emotional energy.

Suggested exercises:

- Emotional Landscape: Draw the terrain of your current state (mountains for stress, storms for grief, open skies for peace)

- Colour Mood Tracking: Track your week using only colour, what does your pattern show?

- Mask Creation: Design your social mask. Then draw what's behind it.

These activities re-integrate parts often marginalised by purely verbal approaches. Art therapy techniques like these are increasingly validated for trauma healing and emotional regulation (Malchiodi, 2012).

Create Here

Collage of the Self

Create a collage using cut-out images, words, colours, and textures that reflect your true identity, not your public performance. This is powerful because it bypasses performance. The collage cannot lie.

Try doing one collage for who you were told to be, and another for who you are becoming.

Reflection prompt: What images did you choose? What did you omit? Why?

Create Here

Symbolic Deconstruction of Media

Select one advertisement, corporate logo, or political poster. Analyse it symbolically:

- What colours are used? What emotions do they evoke?

- What archetypes are being activated?

- What unconscious beliefs is it trying to embed?

This trains symbolic fluency. The more you decode the world's symbols, the more yours become sovereign.

Let this section serve as your return to the visual, where intuition, insight, and imagination intersect. These are not 'activities', they are acts of reclamation.

You are not a machine built only to analyse. You are a being meant to perceive, to feel, to create.

So draw your truth. Colour your contradiction. Decode your story.

This is not an art class. This is a freedom class.

Symbols are the subconscious language of the mind. While words shape thought, symbols shape belief. Visuals bypass analytical resistance and speak directly to emotion, memory, and intuition. This section invites you to explore the symbolic landscape of perception through curated visuals, colour practices, and reflective drawing.

Throughout this book, you've encountered ideas that live in language. Now we render those ideas visible, and, through your engagement, alive.

Create Here

Final Words: The Return to Wholeness

This book is not the conclusion. It is a threshold. A marker. A moment of pause in a world that rarely stops moving.

What you've read is not just my story. It is yours, too, refracted through different moments, different people, and different environments. I have shared what I could, not to provide answers, but to create openings. To hand you a mirror that reflects not just pain or truth, but *potential*, the sacred, often silent potential within every one of us to begin again.

You may have reached this point with questions still unanswered. That's not failure. That's freedom. If even one idea in this book loosened a knot in your mind, softened a rigid belief, helped you reconnect with your true voice, or gave language to an unnamed experience, then it has served its purpose.

You are not broken. The world is not beyond healing. The illusion will continue, but so will the awakening. And within the noise of knowing, your signal can still rise.

Thank you for walking this far with me. May you continue, gently, fiercely, consciously, on your path.

Acknowledgements

To those who misunderstood me, thank you. You taught me to trust my voice.

To those who saw me, even when I couldn't see myself, I am forever grateful. You reminded me I was never truly alone.

To the thinkers, writers, mentors, critics, and strangers whose words moved through me and out of me, this book carries your resonance.

To my children, you are the reason I continue. You are my roots and my wings.

And to the reader, thank you. For your presence. For your openness. For your time. I honour the space you've given this book and the space you continue to reclaim in your own life.

Appendix: Questions for Further Reflection

- What beliefs about yourself were inherited, and which have you earned?
- What roles do you still perform to feel accepted?
- When did you last act from pure intuition, without fear or reward?
- What are you ready to release?
- What are you ready to reclaim?

Suggested Reading & Listening

- *The Myth of Normal* — Dr. Gabor Maté

- *Prometheus Rising* — Robert Anton Wilson

- *The Crowd: A Study of the Popular Mind* — Gustave Le Bon

- *The True Believer* — Eric Hoffer

- *The End of the World is Just the Beginning* — Peter Zeihan

- Podcasts: **Those Conspiracy Guys**, **The Art of Charm**

Use this area to start a Journal or Culminate all your notes from the book in one place.

Disclaimer

This book is a work of non-fiction rooted in personal experience, research, reflection, and independent interpretation of events, systems, and cultural phenomena. The content is intended for educational and informational purposes only and should not be considered professional advice in the fields of mental health, law, spirituality, or science.

The views and perspectives shared herein are the author's own and are not intended to malign any individual, group, organisation, institution, or belief system. Any resemblance to real people, living or dead, or actual events is purely coincidental unless stated otherwise.

Readers are encouraged to apply critical thinking and discernment to all ideas presented. Where controversial or speculative subjects are discussed, they are shared for open exploration, not to assert absolute truth. If you are experiencing emotional or psychological distress, please seek support from a qualified professional.

Use of AI-Generated Content

Portions of this book, including editorial suggestions, image concepts, and structural assistance, were developed in collaboration with **OpenAI's ChatGPT**, a language model trained on publicly available and licensed data. All final content was reviewed and edited by the author to reflect personal intent and lived experience.

All AI-generated images used in this work (if applicable) were created via OpenAI's image tools with full rights granted for commercial and creative use by the author. You may freely include these images in your book and sell the work, as long as your use complies with relevant laws and does not infringe on any third-party rights.

www.ingramcontent.com/pod-product-compliance
Lightning Source LLC
Chambersburg PA
CBHW060519280326
41933CB00014B/3027